Contents

Dolphins in the Wild

by Anna Bunney
illustrated by Jon Hughes

CAMBRIDGE
UNIVERSITY PRESS

UCL
Institute of Education

1. What is a dolphin?

Dolphins are very intelligent marine mammals. They are part of the toothed whale family, along with porpoises, beaked whales and the sperm whale. There are over 40 different kinds of dolphin around the world. They can be found in every ocean on the planet, from the icy cold Arctic to the warm, Caribbean waters, as well as in some of the largest rivers in the world.

Dolphins belong in a group of animals called **cetaceans**. This group includes all whales, dolphins and porpoises.

Dolphins are under **threat** from the activities of man, such as fishing with nets. Some **species** are in danger of **extinction**, unless humans act to save them.

Vaquita

Amazon River Dolphin

Bottlenose Dolphin

White-beaked Dolphin

Dolphins can be found all over the world

Common Dolphin

Short-finned Pilot Whales

Striped Dolphin

Hourglass Dolphin

Hector's Dolphin

3

2. What do dolphins look like?

Dolphins have a curved fin on their back, which is positioned in the middle of their body. This is called a dorsal fin. Most dolphins have a long mouth, called a beak.

Dolphins swim up to the water surface and use their blowhole to breathe air. The blowhole acts like a nose. Dolphins have a single blowhole which is on the top of their head.

Dolphins' **camouflaged** bodies helps them hunt their food. They have dark backs and pale tummies, so if they swim above a group of fish, they blend in with the pale water surface and the sky above. If they swim below a group of fish, their dark backs are camouflaged against the dark sea bed below.

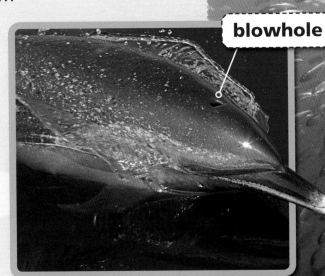

blowhole

Dolphins' tails are called a tail fluke. The tails move up and down to power the dolphin through the water. Dolphins have two pectoral fins. The pectoral fins help them steer.

beak

eye

dorsal fin

pectoral fin

tail fluke

3. Dolphins are mammals

Dolphin Fact:
Baby dolphins are born tail first. Other female dolphins will then push the **calf** safely to the surface of the water for its first breath.

Some people think dolphins are fish because they live in the sea. But they are mammals, just like humans. They have a backbone, breathe oxygen from the air and are warm-blooded.

They give birth to live young, and the young feed on milk from their mother.

All mammals have hair. Dolphins are born with whiskers on their top jaw, which fall out soon after birth.

Dolphin Fact:

Dolphins have to keep their body temperature warm at all times, even when they are swimming in cold seas. To keep them warm, dolphins have a thick layer of fat around their body, called blubber. The blubber acts as insulation, keeping dolphins warm in cold water.

Differences between dolphins and fish

Bottlenose dolphin *Salmon*

Mammal	Fish
Breathes oxygen from the air, using its blowhole	Has gills, which allow it to extract oxygen from the water
Gives birth to live young	Lays eggs
Young feed on mother's milk	Mothers do not look after their young
Tail moves up and down	Tail moves side to side
Born with whiskers	Does not have any hair
Warm-blooded	Cold-blooded

4. Pods and travelling

A group of dolphins is called a pod. The size of a pod varies, but it is usually between two and 20 dolphins. They are very protective of each other and travel in pods for safety in numbers, to deter **predators** such as killer whales. The calves swim in the middle of the pod, so that the adults can protect them. However, dolphins are not always kind towards each other. There can be fighting between members of the pod, and they occasionally pick on weaker dolphins.

Dolphins are **carnivores**, eating mainly fish and squid. They must travel to find food. Sometimes there is a lot of food around and they can stay in one area for a while. Other times, they can travel hundreds of miles to look for food.

When thousands of dolphins gather to feed and travel, a super pod is formed. Super pods have over 1,000 dolphins in them. A super pod is made up of many smaller pods.

This pod is travelling to find food.

5. Communication

Most dolphins have extremely good eyesight. They can see well underwater and out of the water. Dolphins can often be seen spyhopping. This means they will stick their heads out of the water and have a look around.

Sometimes it is very dark and murky underwater. Then it is impossible for them to see. Instead, they will use sound to help them. This is called echolocation. Dolphins use it for finding food, communication and navigation.

They make clicking and squeaking noises in their blowhole. These noises reflect off the back of the dolphin's skull and then shoot forward, passing through an organ inside its head called a melon. The melon is a large, fatty organ which turns the sound into a sound beam. The sound travels through the water and when it hits an object, the echo comes back to the dolphin and tells it about the object: how far away it is, its shape and how big it is.

Dolphins can recognise each other by using sound. Each dolphin has its own sound called a 'signature whistle'. When a calf is born, members of its pod will repeat the signature whistle to the calf until it learns its own **unique** whistle.

6. Dolphins and their relatives

Spinner Dolphins

The Spinner Dolphin is found in warm waters all around the world. These dolphins are well-known for their energetic leaps and spins. They can jump up to three metres into the air, and spin up to seven times before re-entering the water.

Spinner Dolphins swim into deep waters to feed at night, eating fish, squid and shrimps. During the day, they rest in shallow waters, closer to land.

Spinner Dolphin spinning

Spinner Dolphins jumping out of the water

Orcas

Orcas, or killer whales, are not actually whales. They are the largest species of dolphin.

Orcas are excellent hunters and were named killer whales after sailors saw them hunting and eating whales.

There are different types of orcas. Each type is a different size, feed on different prey and live in different sized pods.

Orcas living in Norway are fish eaters. They have a special way of feeding on large schools of herring. First, they herd the herring into tight balls using loud echolocation calls, and swim around the school of fish in circles to trap them. They then slap the fish with their tails to stun them, making them easier to catch and eat.

Large orcas living in Antarctic waters have been seen creating large waves to wash seals off the ice so they can eat them.

Orcas sometimes work together to kill sharks. They only eat the liver, as it contains lots of nutrients.

Where river dolphins are found

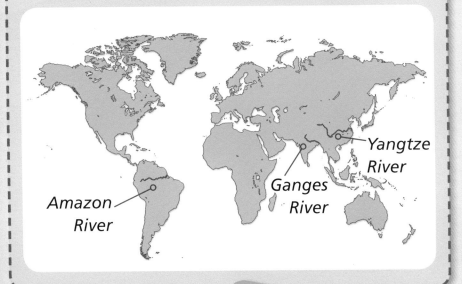

River Dolphins

River dolphins live in **freshwater**, in some of the world's largest rivers, like the Amazon and Ganges.

These rivers are very muddy and murky, and it is difficult to see through the water. So, the river dolphins have to rely on their echolocation to find food, communicate with each other and to navigate. As they do not need their eyesight, the river dolphins are blind.

The Amazon River Dolphin is the largest of the river dolphins. It is sometimes called the Boto. It is pale pink in colour and, unlike other dolphins, has a flexible neck. This allows it to move its head from side to side and up and down. Botos grow up to 3 metres long. They feed on fish, turtles and crabs.

Amazon River Dolphins

one of the last photos of a Yangtze River Dolphin

The Yangtze River Dolphin became extinct very recently. Human activity caused this. The Yangtze River used to be home to thousands of the river dolphins. Fishermen used long, hooked lines and nets to catch fish, but the dolphins got tangled up in them. These dolphins couldn't reach the surface of the water to breathe, so they drowned. Large, noisy ships were allowed to travel up and down the river, making it too noisy for the dolphins to use their echolocation. Without echolocation, they could not find food, navigate or communicate with each other. River Dolphins could not survive.

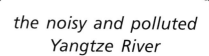

the noisy and polluted Yangtze River

Porpoises

Porpoises are similar to dolphins but are smaller in size. Their dorsal fin is more triangular and they have different shaped teeth.

The Vaquita is the smallest porpoise and the smallest of all the cetaceans. The name Vaquita means 'little cow' in Spanish. It lives only in the Sea of Cortez in Mexico. It is 1.2 metres long – the same height as a six year old child.

The Vaquita is nearly extinct. Scientists think that there are fewer than 30 remaining in the wild. Their small size makes it very easy for them to get caught in fishing nets. They can't swim to the surface to breathe so they drown.

The Harbour Porpoise is the only porpoise found in European waters. The Harbour Porpoise is sometimes called the 'puffing pig' because of the puffing sound it makes when it breathes. The English word 'porpoise' comes from the Latin word for pig – porcus.

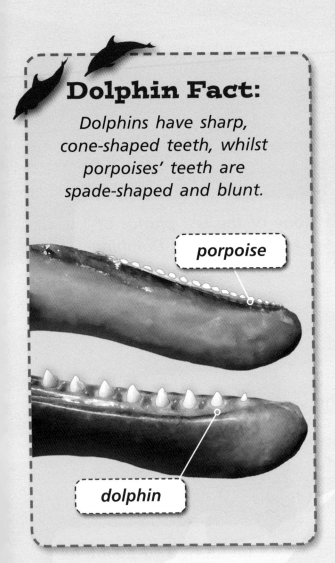

Dolphin Fact:

Dolphins have sharp, cone-shaped teeth, whilst porpoises' teeth are spade-shaped and blunt.

porpoise

dolphin

The six species of porpoise

Burmeister's Porpoise

Finless Porpoise

Harbour Porpoise

Spectacled Porpoise

Vaquita

Dall's Porpoise

19

Hector's Dolphin

Hector's Dolphins are the smallest and rarest marine dolphins in the world. They have black markings on their face, and a dorsal fin shaped like a mouse ear. They are found only in the shallow coastal waters in New Zealand. There are about 8,000 Hector's Dolphins.

Ganges River Dolphin

This dolphin lives in the freshwater rivers of Nepal, India and Bangladesh. It swims on its side so that its pectoral fin digs up the muddy bottom of the river, helping to find food. No one knows how exactly many Ganges River Dolphins are left, but they are endangered.

Northern Right Whale Dolphin

Northern Right Whale Dolphins live in deep water and, unlike other dolphins, they do not have a dorsal fin. They can swim very fast, up to 25 miles per hour in large pods of 100 – 200 dolphins.

Hourglass Dolphin

Hourglass Dolphins are beautiful creatures which get their name from the black and white pattern on their sides. This species is not endangered, and it is estimated that there are about 145,000 Hourglass Dolphins in the world. They live close to Antarctica.

7. Dolphin Life Cycles

Female dolphins give birth to a calf every two to four years. The calf will stay with its mother for at least a year. During that time, the mother will teach it how to hunt, feed and communicate.

Orcas live together as a family. When an orca calf is born, it will stay with its mother in the family pod for its whole life.

Different species of dolphins can live for different lengths of time. The **lifespan** of an orca is around 80 years, but some live to over 100 years. Bottlenose Dolphins live for about 50 years, and Harbour Porpoises for about 12.

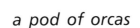

a pod of orcas

marine life food chain

8. Threats

Dolphins are beautiful, intelligent and sociable creatures that benefit the planet greatly. It is important to protect them.

Unfortunately, many dolphins are in danger of extinction. However, there are things that can be done to help stop these threats in the future.

dolphin swimming alongside rubbish

Plastic bags can look like jellyfish, which many marine animals like to eat.

Marine Pollution

A lot of rubbish ends up in the sea. Wind can blow rubbish on the land straight into the sea. The rain washes rubbish into streams, rivers and drains which flow into the sea. Dolphins eat rubbish thinking that it is food, and can choke on it. If they swallow it, their stomachs get so full of rubbish that they are too full to eat any real food and they starve to death.

Noise Pollution

Boat engines, building in the sea and other man-made underwater sounds all make lots of noise. If it's too noisy, dolphins can't use echolocation to navigate, communicate or find food.

Habitat destruction

If a dolphin's habitat gets destroyed, it has nowhere to live. For example, parts of the Amazon River are being destroyed by deforestation and dam building. This results in fewer fish and fewer habitats for the remaining Amazon River Dolphins to live in.

Fishing nets

Many dolphins die in fishermen's nets. Modern fishing nets are made of line that is very strong, but also invisible. The nets catch fish without them being able to see the net coming towards them. However, this means it also catches dolphins. If a dolphin gets caught in a net, it cannot get to the surface of the water to breathe, so it drowns.

Captivity

Lots of people enjoy watching dolphins. But dolphins are often kept in tanks in marine parks. Putting whales and dolphins in tanks for entertainment is wrong. They are very intelligent creatures and they need to live in social groups with their families. Wild dolphins swim hundreds of miles a day, but when in captivity they have little space to swim.

What is the solution?

Some of these threats can be prevented by humans.

- Reduce the amount of waste produced by avoiding buying products with excessive packaging. Use reusable shopping bags.

- Reuse as much as possible. For example, buy water in a reusable bottle and refill from the tap.

- Recycle plastic. This removes the chance that it will be washed into the ocean.

- Make sure no litter is dropped on the floor, as it can easily blow into the sea. Most marine litter originates from the land, not the sea.

- Ask for sustainable fish in supermarkets and at restaurants – these fish are caught using lines and hooks, which is much less damaging to dolphins.

- Go and observe dolphins in the wild instead of in captivity, where they have plenty of space to hunt and play.

9. Preserving dolphins

Dolphins are some of the most beautiful creatures on earth, but they are also very important and need to be protected. They play an important role in keeping the oceans healthy. They do this by eating other animals, mainly fish and squid. Without dolphins, their prey would increase in number by too much. This would mean all of the smaller fish and plants in that area would get eaten.

Dolphins are also a source of food for some other creatures. Without dolphins, their predators wouldn't have as much food to eat and their numbers would fall.

Dolphins help keep the balance between species.

If the ocean was not a healthy habitat with lots of food to eat, the dolphins would not be able to survive. The presence of dolphins is therefore a sign of a healthy environment. By protecting dolphins, humans can help **preserve** healthy marine habitats. This is important because a large number of the world's people rely heavily on the ocean for their food and livelihood.

Dolphins need to swim in a clean, healthy ocean.

Glossary

acrobatic   body movements involving twists and flips

aggression   forceful, angry behaviour

calf   baby dolphin, whale or porpoise

camouflaged   coloured or marked to blend in with the surroundings

captivity   kept out of their natural environment

carnivores   animals which only eat meat

dam   large barrier which is built to hold back water

echo   sound that bounces back to its source after hitting an object

endangered   in danger of extinction

energetic   with great energy and activity

extinct   species that has died out

freshwater   not salty sea water

habitat   natural home of an animal

marine   found in the sea

organ   part of the body which has a specific function

pollution   something added to the environment which has harmful effects

predators   animals which feeds on other animals

preserve   keep something in its original condition

prey   animal that is hunted by other animals for food

reflect   bounce back

remote   place which is located away from human populations

sea bed   bottom of the ocean

schools   group of fish

sociable   friendly, and likes to be around others

species   group of very similar animals

stun   knock something unconscious or make it unable to react

sustainable   activities which meet the needs of people today without damaging the resource for the future.

threat   something likely to cause danger

unique   different from anything else

Index

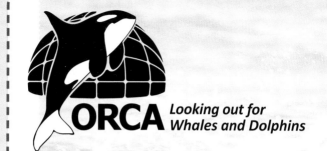

ORCA *Looking out for Whales and Dolphins*

ORCA is a UK whale and dolphin conservation charity dedicated to the long term protection of whales, dolphins and porpoises, and their habitats. ORCA's projects reach people of all ages providing memorable educational activities and local wildlife experiences both on and offshore.

www.orcaweb.org.uk

info@orcaweb.org.uk

Charity number: 1141728

Dolphins in the Wild Anna Bunney

Teaching notes written by Glen Franklin and Sue Bodman

Using this book

Content/theme/subject

Features of non-chronological report and persuasive writing, with some elements of instruction, are used in this mixed genre non-fiction text to explore how dolphins live in the wild, before considering efforts to conserve this endangered species for future generations.

Language structure

- Appropriate voice and register is used: generic voice for reporting sections with direct instructions to the reader regarding preservation of the dolphin population.
- Grammatical choices, such as the use of adverbial words and phrases (*'Unfortunately'*, *'However'*) demonstrate the author's position.

Book structure/visual features

- Appropriate layout and non-fiction design features are employed.
- Dramatic, real-life photographs are interspersed with tables, maps and diagrams to illustrate the messages explored in the main text.

Vocabulary and comprehension

- Subject-specific vocabulary is used appropriately, supported by additional information in facts boxes and a comprehensive glossary.

Curriculum links

Art and Design – Explore and evaluate design and layout of non-fiction texts (including websites), considering how well information is relayed. For example, are there additional features that do not support the facts. Would a chart have aided the reader's understanding?

Learning outcomes

Children can:

- use a range of non-chronological report sources to gather information
- record and present information on a given topic
- consider authorial intent, seeking evidence in the text to support their conclusion.

Planning for guided reading

Lesson One: Gathering information from a range of sources

Note: you will also need a range of information books about dolphins and other marine mammals, or access to internet websites for this lesson.

Activate prior knowledge by discussing what the children know already about dolphins. Establish that dolphins are marine mammals, like whales and porpoises. Also, that they are endangered. Most children will be familiar with the features of non-fiction texts by Strand 3, but check and revise any aspects with which they are unsure.

Children read p.2 quietly to themselves to establish what a dolphin is. There are four glossary words on this page. Check together to establish their meaning.

Now turn to the contents page. Remind children that non-fiction books are used to find information related to an area of investigation. Demonstrate selecting an area of interest: *I think I read somewhere that dolphins can talk to each other. I wonder if that is really true? Let's look in the section on communication. Turn to p.10.* Explore the technical vocabulary, such as *'echolocation'*, and ensure children understand the meaning from reading the text.

Set an independent reading task. Ask children to choose an aspect of the topic they wish to read about. For example, a particular dolphin relative such as River Dolphins or Orcas. Have them make notes to summarise the key facts they found out in